How to Use Digital Tools to Support Teachers in a PLC

William M. Ferriter

Solution Tree | Press

555 North Morton Street
Bloomington, IN 47404
800.733.6786 (toll free) / 812.336.7700
FAX: 812.336.7790
email: info@solution-tree.com
solution-tree.com

Visit **go.solution-tree.com/PLCbooks** to access the links mentioned in this book.

Printed in the United States of America

19 18 17 16 15   1 2 3 4 5

Library of Congress Cataloging-in-Publication Data

Ferriter, William M.
  How to use digital tools to support teachers in a PLC / William M. Ferriter.
    pages cm -- (Solutions)
  Includes bibliographical references.
  ISBN 978-1-942496-00-7 (perfect bound) 1. Professional learning communities.
2. Professional learning communities--Computer networks. 3. Teachers--In-service
training--Computer networks. 4. Mentoring in education--Computer networks. I. Title.
  LB1738.F48 2015
  370.71'1--dc23
                            2015004803

Solution Tree
Jeffrey C. Jones, CEO
Edmund M. Ackerman, President

Solution Tree Press
President: Douglas M. Rife
Associate Acquisitions Editor: Kari Gillesse
Editorial Director: Lesley Bolton
Managing Production Editor: Caroline Weiss
Copy Editor: Ashante K. Thomas
Proofreader: Elisabeth Abrams
Text and Cover Designer: Rian Anderson
Compositor: Rachel Smith

This book is dedicated to Rick and Becky DuFour—two amazing people who leave me inspired, hopeful, and confident that, working together, we CAN create the learning spaces that our students deserve.

Visit **go.solution-tree.com/PLCbooks** to access the links mentioned in this book.

Table of Contents

About the Author

 **William M. Ferriter** is a National Board Certified Teacher of sixth graders in a professional learning community (PLC) in Raleigh, North Carolina. He has designed professional development courses for educators throughout the United States. He is also a founding member and senior fellow of the Teacher Leaders Network and has served as teacher in residence at the Center for Teaching Quality.

An advocate for PLCs, student-centered learning spaces, improved teacher working conditions, and teacher leadership, Bill has represented educators on Capitol Hill and presented at state, national, and international conferences. He has also had articles published in the *Journal for Staff Development*, *Educational Leadership*, *Phi Delta Kappan*, and *Threshold Magazine*. A contributing author to two assessment anthologies, *The Teacher as Assessment Leader* and *The Principal as Assessment Leader*, he is also coauthor of *Communicating and Connecting With Social Media*, *Building a Professional Learning Community at Work*™, *Making Teamwork Meaningful*, and *Teaching the iGeneration* (Second Edition).

Bill earned a bachelor of science and master of science in elementary education from the State University of New York at Geneseo. To learn more about Bill's work, visit http://blog.williamferriter.com or follow @plugusin on Twitter.

To book Bill Ferriter for professional development, contact pd@solution-tree.com.

Introduction

Ask anyone who has spent the better part of his or her career as an educator, and that person will tell you that teaching in today's classrooms can feel like an almost impossible challenge. Our schools have become increasingly diverse—socially, economically, *and* academically. Students who are struggling with poverty, struggling to learn new languages, and struggling to believe in the intentions of communities that have all too often left them disaffected and disengaged sit alongside students who have mastered essential content before the academic year even begins. Complicating matters is the fact that society *expects more* from graduates than ever before. Gone are the days when memorizing individual facts and figures was enough for students to earn diplomas. Instead, new sets of standards detailed by both public and private organizations—national and provincial governments, state legislatures, councils of political leaders, organizations that represent the interests of leaders in science, business, and industry—demand that every student leaves our schools ready to evaluate, persuade, influence, analyze, and synthesize at the highest levels (National Governors Association Center for Best Practices & Council of Chief State School Officers, 2010; NGSS Lead States, 2013; Partnership for 21st Century Skills, 2009).

Our students are also changing. Having grown up in a fast-paced world where technology makes constant participation possible, they see traditional schools as irrelevant. Engagement drops year after year as students realize that the independent, self-selected, passion-based learning they do beyond schools bears little resemblance to the

1

teacher-directed, presentation-heavy, one-size-fits-all learning that continues to define our buildings (Busteed, 2013). Preparing dozens of dissatisfied students with unique sets of strengths and weaknesses to succeed in tomorrow's world can overwhelm anyone working alone. "The only thing worse than being bored," educational change expert Michael Fullan (2013) writes in *Stratosphere*, "is being responsible for teaching the bored under conditions that restrict what you can do" (p. 17).

That's where the power and promise of professional learning communities (PLCs) come in. The simple truth is that teachers no longer *have* to work alone. Collaborating to collectively define the knowledge and skills that are essential for students to master and then working together to identify and amplify high-leverage instructional practices empowers everyone. Teachers who have figured out the keys to student engagement can share strategies with peers who are struggling in disconnected classrooms. Teachers who are skilled at integrating higher-order thinking skills into daily lessons can lift peers who are struggling with the transition to classrooms where knowing isn't as important as doing, and teachers with a deep and meaningful understanding of their content areas can lend a hand to colleagues who are struggling to identify the kinds of curricular misconceptions that commonly confuse students.

However, collaboration isn't as easy as it sounds because it requires a measure of coordination between colleagues that teachers in traditional schools aren't used to. Tasks that were once completed in isolation—identifying essential content and skills, developing and delivering assessments, taking action on behalf of students struggling to master the core curriculum or in need of enrichment—become tasks that are completed with partners. Information that teachers once managed themselves—lesson plans, unit-overview sheets, data sets communicating evidence of student progress—becomes information that has to be efficiently communicated to others. Even the students in our classrooms—who have always been seen as the responsibility of individual teachers—are shared in professional learning communities as teachers work to give every student access to the expertise of the entire team.

While teachers are rarely opposed to the notion of coordinating their work, coordination *does* take additional time, energy, and effort. In organizational theory, time, energy, and effort are called a transaction cost (Shirky, 2008). Every additional planning meeting designed to bring members together, every additional email generated to organize team choices, every additional minute spent looking for shared documents, and every additional moment spent wrestling to come to consensus or to reorganize students to meet their individual needs is a transaction cost—and teachers in professional learning communities will inevitably weigh the perceived benefits of shared tasks against collaboration's mental and physical demands before changing their behaviors. Teachers may believe that collaboration *can* make them stronger, but they won't begin to work together in meaningful ways until they are convinced that the kinds of core tasks that PLCs embrace are *doable*.

The good news is that new digital tools can make coordination in knowledge-driven workspaces easier. Whether that coordination depends on the sharing of ideas, having deeper conversations about important issues, creating shared work products, or taking action around knotty issues, digital tools are fundamentally changing the way we work together. On a large scale, people around the world are organizing themselves in online spaces that are designed to offer just-in-time support to one another. They share ideas and resources using tools like Twitter (www.twitter.com), develop content with one another using tools like Google Drive (http://drive.google.com), and meet virtually using tools like Skype (www.skype.com) and Google Hangouts (http://hangouts.google.com). Popular social platforms like Facebook and Google+ become homes for interest-specific communities and online conferences covering topics from healthcare and hospice to information security and city management, giving professionals in any field ready access to the hearts and minds of like-minded peers.

Not surprisingly, similar patterns of group behavior exist within schools—most learning teams share ideas and resources with one another to start their collaborative efforts and end by taking action together (Graham & Ferriter, 2008). That means the same digital tools that help professionals reimagine learning spaces and coordinate work *beyond* the schoolhouse can be used to facilitate the collective efforts of groups *within* the schoolhouse, lowering transaction costs and convincing teachers that the kinds of practices required of colleagues in professional learning communities are worth tackling.

In *How to Use Digital Tools to Support Teachers in a PLC*, we will take a closer look at just how that work can be done. Each chapter focuses on one of the three increasingly complex collaborative practices that Clay Shirky (2008) details in his seminal work on the impact that digital tools have on the work of groups, *Here Comes Everybody*: (1) sharing, (2) cooperating, and (3) taking collective action. Readers will build awareness of what sharing, cooperating, and taking collective action look like and then explore digital tools that can help make those practices more approachable for PLC members. There is no one right way to read *How to Use Digital Tools to Support Teachers in a PLC*. Some readers will start at page one and work to the end of the text in order to get a sense of the full range of PLC tasks that digital tools can support. Others will read individual chapters addressing the specific collaborative challenges that they are wrestling with.

To help you decide on a strategy that is right for you, here is an overview of the three chapters.

Chapter 1: Sharing

At any given moment, teachers are stumbling across remarkable resources on the web. Whether it is a collection of lessons published by a public television station in the Bay Area of California, a video on bullying produced by high school students in Philadelphia, or a research report released by a national organization detailing the kinds of schools that students most desire, each individual discovery has the potential to spark conversation, improve practice, and change teaching and learning for the better. The challenge for learning communities is aggregating this information—organizing and then sharing it publicly in a way others can easily find. In chapter 1, you will learn to meet this challenge using popular digital tools.

Chapter 2: Cooperating

While sharing requires little real investment on the part of participants, cooperation depends on willing partners who are ready to align their practices with one another. This kind of cooperation within a PLC depends on the ability to come to consensus around shared decisions. Cooperation also depends on collaborative production: together, we need to create content that we are ready to use in our work with students. Coming to consensus around shared decisions and collaboratively producing content, however, can be time-consuming practices simply because they involve negotiated behavior. You can't work as an individual when you are cooperating. Chapter 2 shows you how to facilitate cooperation using digital tools that foster teamwork.

Chapter 3: Taking Collective Action

Collective action is the most sophisticated collaborative behavior in a PLC because it depends on a willingness of all members to honor the will of the group. "Information sharing produces shared awareness among the participants and collaborative production relies on shared creation," explains Shirky (2008), "but collective action creates shared responsibility by tying the user's identity to the identity of the group" (Kindle location 702). In a PLC, collective action begins by building cohesion—a shared sense of what we believe as a group. Collective action then moves into more sophisticated, learning-centered practices as teachers work together to make sure that all students on a grade level or in an academic department master essential outcomes regardless of who their primary teachers are. Chapter 3 details this process and highlights tools that support it.

Author's Note

It is important to note that while the print version of *How to Use Digital Tools to Support Teachers in a PLC* includes suggested tools for helping learning teams share, cooperate, and take collective action, you can always visit http://bit.ly/UDTquickguide to find a constantly updated list of tools and services to use to support the essential skills this book outlines. My goal for extending the *How to Use Digital Tools to Support Teachers in a PLC* collection to the web is to ensure that the content in the print version of this text remains relevant even as popular tools and services change over time.

It is also important to note that there is nothing revolutionary about the tools *How to Use Digital Tools to Support Teachers in a PLC* introduces. In fact, if you constantly find yourself standing at the cutting edge of educational technology, you may well be disappointed by the fact that the tools and suggestions inside this text are functional instead of fantastic. That's intentional, however: when choosing digital tools to support *collaborative* practices, your primary goal should be to find services and solutions that are approachable to *everyone*—not just the most tech-savvy members of your learning communities. As you are reading, keep in mind the teachers on your team who struggle with technology and be on the lookout for processes, practices, and products that they can master easily.

Regardless of how you choose to tackle *How to Use Digital Tools to Support Teachers in a PLC*, commit yourself to finding at least one core practice that you can improve together with your colleagues. Whether you develop a new approach to organizing web-based resources that can move your learning team forward, create digital conversations that allow members of your school community to build consensus around shared directions, or find new ways to track progress by student and standard with products that can automate the collection and analysis of assessment results, *take action*.

The students in your classrooms are counting on you.

Chapter 1
Sharing

Coney Island—the legendary American amusement park that opened in 1880 outside of New York City—is known for everything from remarkable roller coasters and majestic Ferris wheels to hot dog eating contests and carnival-style sideshows. For millions of New York City hipsters, however, Coney Island is best known for its Mermaid Parade held on the last Saturday in June. The annual parade is described on Coney Island's website as "a celebration of ancient mythology and honky-tonk rituals of the seaside" (Coney Island USA, n.d.), where participants don costumes that range from the innocent to the extreme. Stately Aquamen and beautiful Ariels walk alongside scantily clad women shaded by turquoise mermen carrying bedazzled parasols in front of thousands of picture-taking visitors in what is seen as the official start of summer in the beachside community (Shirky, 2008).

For years, pictures of those participants remained in individual collections largely unavailable for public viewing. Sure, small handfuls of high-quality shots taken by professional photographers ended up in magazines and newspapers. Yet because there were no easy ways to share photos in the latter parts of the 20th century, the best Mermaid Parade images taken by locals and tourists alike remained undiscovered. That barrier disappeared in 2004, when Flickr (www.flickr.com)—one of the world's first photo-sharing services—was founded. Designed to make it easy for loosely connected individuals—strangers at a popular parade, fans at the concert of an up-and-coming pop superstar, visitors at sites of historical or cultural significance—to share personal photos, Flickr changed everything for the Mermaid Parade. Without any external coaching or direction from the planners of the Coney Island event or Flickr's owners, folks at the 2005 parade started to upload their best pictures to the service, adding tags—common labels designed to make searching in online spaces easy—in order to create an organized collection of thousands of images that were publicly accessible to anyone with an Internet connection (Shirky, 2008). "The basic capabilities of tools like Flickr reverse the old order of group activity, transforming 'gather, then share' into 'share, then gather,'" Shirky writes (2008, Kindle location 513).

That same reversal—share, then gather—is now changing the way teachers organize. Whether they are using microblogging services to sift through the online finds of like-minded strangers or systematically building collections of web links with peers that they work with in person, teachers have discovered that digital tools can make sharing—one of the most approachable collaborative practices— easier for everyone.

Finding Sources of Professional Challenge and Inspiration

One of the best examples of the benefits of sharing first and gathering later in education is the groups of connected educators curating content for one another on Twitter (www.twitter.com), a social space that often serves as an entry point for any teacher interested in exploring the impact that digital tools can have on collaborative practice. Users who spot potentially valuable resources in online spaces—blog entries, research reports, student project samples, lesson plans, provocative videos—can publicly broadcast what they are finding in short, 140-character messages, called tweets, with one click of a browser-based button. While individual messages are often shared *without* intentionality—users are generally not concerned with who sees the content that they post to Twitter—each message draws attention to useful content, which has the potential to save others time, energy, and effort.

Shirky (2008) argues that reducing the barriers to sharing allows tools like Twitter to make it possible for latent groups to "self-synchronize" (Kindle location 540). Because the perceived value of sharing websites with one another has always been low, large groups of users with shared interests—think teachers—never bothered to invest time and energy into organizing the online content that they were finding for one another. However, Twitter makes sharing websites easy, increasing the perceived benefits of the practice in the eyes of users. When sharing—and discovering the shares of others—becomes a one-click process, it also becomes a collaborative behavior that we are more likely to embrace.

Self-synchronization becomes even more powerful for educators when users start adding hashtags to their Twitter posts. *Hashtags*—like the labels added to Flickr images that made organizing Mermaid Parade photos possible—are unique identifiers added to the end of individual tweets. They typically start with the # symbol and are followed by a short phrase indicating the kind of content that is being shared. Messages that include content connected to PLCs, for example, are tagged #atplc. Messages that include content connected to educational technology are tagged #edtech. Messages that include content connected to school leadership are tagged #cpchat, and messages that include content connected to global education are tagged #globaled.

When users add hashtags to posts in Twitter, others can search for and find their tweets. Teachers of a specific grade level like kindergarten (#kinderchat) are using hashtags to organize content for one another in Twitter. So are teachers working in unique subject areas (#physed), teachers working in entire states and countries (#txed,

#aussieED), and teachers with particular interests (#geniushour). That means any teacher—regardless of grade level, content area, or professional passion—can search Twitter (www.twitter.com/search) to find valuable resources. By making it easy to access a constantly updated stream of resources connected to teaching and learning, Twitter can serve as a source of instructional support and intellectual challenge for PLC members. Revising and reflecting on instructional practices—behaviors that define the work of the most effective learning teams—starts with exposure to new ideas and outside evidence.

Twitter can become much more than a ready source for finding web-based resources, though. Over time, Twitter can also become a ready source for finding new colleagues to learn alongside and to lean on. As teachers begin to follow streams of messages connected to their individual interests, they inevitably spot individuals who are regularly sharing content that resonates. With little effort—replying to other teachers in Twitter is also a one-click process—members of learning teams can reach out and establish new partnerships with teachers who are studying the same topics. While the interactions in Twitter are often superficial—cooperation and collective action can't happen 140 characters at a time—interactions in Twitter can lay the groundwork for more meaningful connections outside of the platform. It is not at all unusual for seasoned Twitter users to turn to members of their digital network when they have questions or need inspiration.

Taking advantage of Twitter's sharing power depends on the following reminders.

Remember to Follow Users With Similar Interests as Yours

One of the easiest ways to access quality content in Twitter is to "follow" other users. When you choose to follow other users, the messages that they post will be added to the time line on your

Twitter home page. That means the choices you make about *who* to follow are incredibly important. Fill your home page with people teaching similar grade levels, content areas, or both, and you are bound to find useful content every time you log in. Fill your home page with people working outside of your field, and you are bound to waste time sifting through irrelevant resources in order to find anything of value.

Remember to Find and Follow Hashtags Connected to Your Interests

While following folks teaching similar grade levels and content areas can provide ready access to quality web finds, don't forget to find and follow hashtags that are connected to your interests as well. Following hashtags can help you spot content and trends in your field that resonate with broad audiences. Following hashtags can also help you spot new partners that are worth learning from. The best place to identify hashtags being used by teachers in similar grade levels or content areas is a list by retired New York City media specialist Jerry Blumengarten titled "Some Educational Hashtags" that can be found online at http://bit.ly/edhashtags. "The Weekly Twitter Chat Schedule" maintained by educational technologist Tom Murray can point you to hashtags that are used for regularly scheduled Twitter chats around specific topics. It can be found online at http://bit.ly/officialchatlist.

Remember That Reading Every Message Is Impossible

Every day, Twitter users post five hundred million messages. That translates to about 350,000 messages per minute (Internet Live Stats, 2014). Even for individual users following small numbers of people or hashtags, the volume of content shared can seem overwhelming. Making Twitter manageable depends on remembering that it is impossible to read every message posted every day. Instead, think of Twitter as a place to turn to when you have a few spare minutes and are looking for something interesting to explore. Concentrate on the value of the content that you *are discovering* instead of on the content that you *may have missed.*

Remember That Sharing Content Is as Important as Finding Content Others Share

The overall health of any social space is dependent on users who are willing to give as much as they take. In spaces like Twitter, that means it is important for every user—including you—to take the time to post resources and ideas for others. Never doubt the value of what you have to share. Embrace the notion that there are teachers who can benefit from any resource that you thought was beneficial. In the end, sharing costs you nothing, so why not make it a regular part of your digital-consumption practices?

Teachers who master Twitter are almost always impressed by and thankful for the service because it provides a constant source of new ideas to explore and new individuals to learn alongside. It is just as important, however, for teachers to find ways to facilitate sharing with the members of their actual learning team.

Organizing Comprehensive Collections of Web-Based Resources

While the content found through Twitter can be incredibly valuable, it can also feel scattered simply because you never know exactly what you will find when logging in. Some days, you might stumble across the perfect lesson for a unit that you have already taught. Other days, you might discover an engaging resource for a project that your students won't tackle until the next semester. Serendipitous discoveries like these are almost always useful, but they aren't always *immediately useful.* That's where social bookmarking applications come into play.

Social bookmarking applications allow users to work together in groups to build organized collections of web-based bookmarks.

For members of PLCs, this can be incredibly valuable. Unlike the loose connections between Twitter users, where the folks you follow often have no real idea what you are trying to teach on a regular basis, the members of your learning team have contextual understandings—an awareness of your curriculum, a sense of your pacing, a recognition of the unique student needs in your school community—that make their web finds more useful to you. Diigo (www.diigo.com)—one of the web's most popular social bookmarking applications—can help you organize these finds in logical ways.

In its simplest form, Diigo works a lot like Twitter: Users click on buttons in their web browser to share content found in online spaces. Resources that are shared can also be tagged, making it easy to build sorted collections that can be searched efficiently. Finally, Diigo bookmarks are stored on the web, making them accessible from any Internet-connected computer—a simple feature that can have real value in buildings where teachers work from several different computers during the course of a school day.

Diigo becomes powerful in PLCs when learning teams work together to decide on the kind of content that will be added to bookmark collections and make plans about how those collections will be organized. Most teams sort web-based resources by unit of study. Some may also sort by school initiative, district initiative, or both—think response to intervention, positive behavior interventions and supports, or project-based learning. Doing so makes it possible for teachers who are looking for useful resources to turn first to content curated by peers teaching the same subjects and working to implement the same initiatives. Instead of sifting through links that *might be useful*, teachers building comprehensive collections of resources together in Diigo know that the content in their shared collection *has been useful* to one of their colleagues.

Diigo collections are often a vast improvement over the traditional strategies learning teams use to share web links with one another. Instead of emailing great finds to one another, adding new sources to paper-based lists maintained by individual teachers, or hunting down colleagues for reminders of content used in previous years—practices that carry high transaction costs for everyone involved—teams that make social bookmarking a collaborative norm fall into efficient patterns where resources are bookmarked, sorted, and shared with everyone all at the same time. Individual teachers can choose to receive email notifications every time a colleague posts a new resource, can choose to receive one email notification per week summarizing all of the shares added to a team's collection, or can choose to simply visit Diigo on the web whenever they are looking for content connected to their current unit of study.

The following tips can help make Diigo work for your learning team.

Create a Group in Diigo for Your Learning Team

One of the reasons that Diigo is such a popular social bookmarking application is that users can create invitation-only groups that can be used to build closed collections of resources. For learning teams, this makes a lot of sense. Creating a Diigo group that includes just the members of your grade-level learning team or subject-specific department means that you can control the content added to your shared collection. While this may mean that your team has access to fewer resources than Diigo users who create public groups with hundreds of members working in schools across the world, a smaller collection of high-quality resources filtered by peers that you work with in person is almost always easier to navigate—and collections that are easier to navigate will save you time.

Create a Common Tagging Language

The key to searching and sorting in social bookmarking applications like Diigo is the tags that users add to individual bookmarks. Essentially, each tag becomes a category in your growing collection of web-based resources. Teachers using Diigo to organize *their own* web finds often add multiple tags to individual resources that represent the complete range of ways that they are likely to remember a site. For example, a news article from CNN on NASA's efforts to study Mars might be tagged "mars," "NASA," "CNN," and "space exploration." However, it is essential to decide in advance on shared tags for individual topics and units of study when teachers are working together to organize resources. If teachers building shared collections of web-based resources fail to use the same tag when sorting bookmarks into categories—think one teacher using "ecology" and another using "natural selection" when bookmarking sites about the Galapagos Islands—finding useful content becomes a frustrating waste of time.

So sit down together and brainstorm a list of tags to use for the content that you are likely to find, add them to Diigo's tag dictionary for your learning team, and make a commitment to one another to use your common tags for every resource added to your shared collection. Common tags for learning teams often start with a short phrase indicating the name of the team's school, grade level, and subject area and end with the name of the unit that a bookmark supports. At Salem Middle School in Apex, North Carolina, for example, the sixth-grade science teachers use the following tags to organize the content in their shared collection.

- salem6sci_matter
- salem6sci_energy
- salem6sci_lithosphere
- salem6sci_space
- salem6sci_ecology
- salem6sci_adaptations

While you can always add individual tags to a link that you plan to share with peers—there is no limit to the number of categories that Diigo can sort resources into—remembering to include the tags that your learning team has agreed on in advance ensures that everyone will be able to find content in your shared collection quickly.

Include Written Descriptions for Every Link

Each time that users bookmark websites in Diigo, they are given the option of adding short written descriptions to their bookmarks. While this may seem like an extra step that makes bookmarking more time consuming, written descriptions are the best way to ensure that your shared collection of web-based resources will be useful to your learning team. Two- or three-sentence descriptions that give a brief overview of the content of a bookmarked site—or of the way that a site can be used to support classroom instruction—can help peers make good choices about resources that are worth exploring. That means the time that *you spend* writing descriptions is time that *your peers will later save* as they sift through your learning team's library of shared resources.

Set Aside Time to Clean and Polish Your Resource Collection

Just like our living rooms, kitchen tables, and nightstands, shared resource collections built with social bookmarking applications like Diigo can become cluttered over time. Teachers who are in a hurry may drop new links into collections without adding common hashtags or written descriptions. Similarly, busy teachers may stumble across great finds that never get added to shared collections at all. Spending twenty to thirty minutes at least once a month working together to add tags, craft written descriptions, delete sites that are no longer useful, and add sites that never ended up in Diigo can help ensure that your shared collection remains a valuable resource for your learning team.

Teach Students to Use Diigo for Shared Research Projects

Another reason that Diigo is one of the most popular social bookmarking applications for educators is that it makes it possible for teachers at any grade level to import class lists and create individual accounts for their students. That means groups of students studying similar topics can begin building shared resource collections, too—mirroring the information-management strategies their teachers embrace. Introducing Diigo to your students can help reinforce your learning team's collaborative efforts: your team will be less likely to give up on social bookmarking if it is a collaborative practice that members are using in their classrooms.

Conclusion

Because sharing is a relatively simple behavior that requires little of individuals outside of being willing to point out valuable resources to peers, its value as a collaborative practice in PLCs can often be underestimated. School change expert Mike Schmoker (2004) writes,

> Mere collegiality won't cut it. Even discussions about curricular issues or popular strategies can feel good but go nowhere. The right image to embrace is of a group of teachers who meet regularly to share, refine, and assess the impact of lessons and strategies continuously to help increasing numbers of students learn at higher levels.

What can't be underestimated, however, is the role that sharing can play in building momentum for learning teams. Asking teachers to demonstrate collaborative persistence in the face of challenging tasks like refining and assessing the impact of their lessons depends on demonstrating early and often that collective efforts can pay real dividends. When teachers recognize that working together can save time—a common discovery made by anyone using social-sharing tools like Twitter or Diigo to find and organize resources and ideas with one another—they are far more likely to believe that more meaningful collaborative practices are doable. Better yet, when teachers use social-sharing tools like Twitter and Diigo to lower the transaction costs tied to basic behaviors like finding and organizing valuable resources and ideas, they can reinvest the time saved into more significant collective efforts centered on helping every student master essential content.

Chapter 2
Cooperating

While it may surprise you, Wikipedia—the popular online encyclopedia created by complete strangers working together with little formal guidance and no real reward—is one of the world's best examples of cooperation in action. Need proof? Consider that since its inception in 2001, almost five million articles have been created in the English version of Wikipedia and that a thousand new articles are added to that collection *every single day*. Those articles are maintained by thirty-five thousand active editors who make nearly three million edits per month (Wikimedia Foundation, 2014). Perhaps the best proof of Wikipedia's success: year after year, it makes the list of the top ten most visited web destinations—a remarkable accomplishment for a site selling nothing and giving everything away for free (Alexa, 2014).

What many people don't know, however, is that Wikipedia's early efforts at cooperation were nothing short of a miserable failure. First imagined by Jimmy Wales and Larry Sanger in early 2000, Wikipedia's original iteration, Nupedia, was designed as a free online encyclopedia created and maintained by *experts*. "Suppose scholars the world over were to learn of a serious online encyclopedia effort in which the results were not proprietary to the encyclopedists. How quickly would the encyclopedia grow?" ask Wales and Sanger (as cited in Shirky, 2008, Kindle location 1396).

Unlike Wikipedia's free-flowing style where literally anyone with Internet access can work together to create and edit articles, Nupedia articles were each written by one author and carefully reviewed for accuracy by an editorial board before any content was posted. At any point in the review process, an article could be stopped and returned to its author for corrections. Errors ranging from simple spelling and grammar mistakes to significant content inaccuracies could derail progress toward publishing anything on Nupedia. The review process was so thorough—and so cumbersome—that after months of initial work, Nupedia had less than twenty finished articles on its site (Shirky, 2008).

To speed this review process, Sanger—who was serving as Nupedia's editor in chief—used a wiki service to create Wikipedia as a place where initial drafts of Nupedia articles could be posted and revised. Access to Wikipedia was opened to anyone with content to share, and Sanger—hoping to prove that an expedited revision process could produce content quickly—encouraged Nupedia community members and experts to spend just a few minutes adding content to the new site. Within weeks, Wikipedia had more articles—and higher-quality articles—than Nupedia had been able to produce in months. By the end of the year, Nupedia disappeared and Wikipedia had become a remarkable example of the role that digital tools could play in helping people cooperate around the creation of shared content (Shirky, 2008).

What lessons can professional learning communities learn from Wikipedia's success and Nupedia's demise? First, the collaborative production of content is a more sophisticated group process than the sharing practices explored in chapter 1. Shirky (2008) writes,

> Collaborative production can be valuable, but it is harder to get right than sharing, because anything that has to be negotiated about, like a Wikipedia article, takes more energy than things that can just be accreted, like a group of photos. (Kindle location 695)

Second, traditional barriers to the collaborative production of content—the kinds of rigid processes put in place to govern the work of Nupedia—can discourage cooperation. Nupedia's experts and authors realized that the time, energy, and effort it took to get articles published on the site far outweighed the perceived value of the work that they were doing. Finally, digital tools can make it easier for groups to create, revise, and improve on shared content. Wikipedia articles may not be perfect on the day that they are created, but improvement is a given—the result of the efforts of editors who are working together without frustration thanks to digital tools.

Successful Negotiating in PLCs

One of the core beliefs in professional learning communities is that teachers should collaborate on matters related to student learning. PLCs are invested in the notion that it is fundamentally impossible to help *all students* learn unless *all teachers* are willing to work together. They realize that the collective experience of the group trumps the individual expertise of teachers working alone. "Teams in a PLC relentlessly question the status quo, seek new methods of teaching and learning, test the methods, and then reflect on the results," write PLC experts Richard DuFour, Rebecca DuFour, and Robert Eaker. "Building shared knowledge of both current reality and best practice is an essential part of each team's decision-making process" (DuFour, DuFour, & Eaker, n.d.).

All of these behaviors—building shared knowledge, questioning the status quo, seeking new methods of teaching and learning, testing those methods, and reflecting on results together—depend on cooperation and result in the collaborative production of content. Together, teachers on learning teams must develop shared instructional materials—overview sheets, sets of essential outcomes, lesson plans, common assessments—for each unit. Since inquiry around what works best for students is a never-ending process, teachers on learning teams must also *continue* to reflect on and improve the content that they create together.

Like every entry created for Wikipedia, however, reflecting on and improving shared content in a professional learning community often depends on successful negotiations between individual teachers over just what should be included in final products. Developing lists of essential outcomes requires teams to have conversations around what students should know and be able to do at the end of each unit. Shared lesson plans can only be created after teams agree on the kinds of instructional strategies that resonate with students. Common assessments will only be embraced once teachers have a mutual definition of what responsible assessment looks like in action.

Successful negotiations over issues like essential outcomes, effective instruction, and responsible assessment start only once every member of a professional learning team has ample opportunities to give input and to express disagreement in a safe way. While these kinds of negotiations are best held during the course of regularly scheduled meetings where members can read the body language and hear the tone of voice of their peers, there are a range of digital tools that can be used to indicate early starting points for shared decisions. Two tools that are currently popular are AnswerGarden and Tricider.

AnswerGarden (http://answergarden.ch) allows users to easily collect the thoughts and reflections of groups. With just a few simple clicks, users can create interactive online spaces where participants can add text responses to any question or topic. New responses show up automatically in an AnswerGarden, giving members a public sense of their peers' opinions. Users can also vote for others' ideas simply by clicking on and resubmitting responses that already appear in an AnswerGarden. Like Wordle, responses that receive multiple votes in an AnswerGarden grow in size, making it possible for teams to quickly identify ideas with significant traction.

While AnswerGarden allows users to password protect the interactive spaces that they create and to moderate any responses before they can be seen by others, it is more useful as a collaborative tool when password-protection features aren't enabled simply because passwords and comment moderation add unnecessary transaction costs to the process of gathering feedback.

Designed to help teams make decisions about specific strategies that are worth pursuing, Tricider (www.tricider.com) takes collaborative brainstorming around complex issues one step further. After a question with multiple potential answers to consider has been generated—think "What is the best way to reach reluctant readers?" or "What tool should we use to organize the content that we create together?"—Tricider allows users to post new ideas that may be worth pursuing. For as long as a Tricider conversation (called a tricision) remains active, users can add pros and cons to existing ideas and vote for ideas that they think have merit. Like AnswerGarden, Tricider conversations can be password protected. This is not recommended, however, simply because password protections make it harder for participants to share their thinking. *Someone* is going to lose his or her password the minute it is created and feel left out of the conversation.

Learning teams can use AnswerGarden and Tricider to quickly identify areas of overlap in the initial thinking of individual members. Interested in how teachers are feeling about the nonfiction reading strategies that you are incorporating into your social studies classrooms? Create an AnswerGarden and start asking for opinions. Ready to discuss the best way to teach students to multiply fractions? List a few common practices and do some light voting in Tricider. Because adding thoughts and ideas to AnswerGarden and Tricider requires little time or technical skill, every member of your learning team *will be able to* participate. More importantly, because adding thoughts and ideas to AnswerGarden and Tricider can be done anonymously, every member of your learning team *will be willing to* participate. As a result, successful negotiations over important decisions can become a regular part of your learning team's practice.

Moving From Negotiations to the Collaborative Production of Content in PLCs

Moving from negotiations to collaborative production in PLCs—the next step in mastering cooperation as a group behavior—depends on approachable structures and processes for developing and organizing shared content. Everyone has to be able to easily find materials that teams are developing together. Everyone also has to have the technical skill to add to shared files. If members feel like they can't easily make contributions to the content that their peers create or if producing shared content becomes a time-consuming or technically challenging process, teachers will quickly walk away from collaborative production no matter how valuable it may be.

One of the best tools for supporting collaborative production is Google Drive (www.google.com/drive/). In its simplest form, Google Drive is a cloud storage service offered to anyone with a free Google account. Literally anything—documents, PowerPoint presentations, photos, videos—can be uploaded to your Google Drive. Storing content in Google Drive instead of on jump drives or on computer hard drives makes content that was once tied to individual devices portable. You can access resources stored in the cloud from any device. Google Drive users can also add a dedicated folder to computers, phones, and tablets that automatically syncs to both the web and to other machines. Create a new handout during a planning period at school? Write a retest for struggling students while working at home? As long as those revisions are saved inside of the Google Drive folder on the computer that you are using, they will instantly appear in both your Google Drive account online and on any other computer where you have installed a Google Drive folder.

This kind of instant syncing can be invaluable to individuals largely because it provides peace of mind. No longer do you have to worry about losing any of the content you create. If you wake one morning to find that your school computer has been unexpectedly reimaged by district technology officials who are updating operating systems or you return home one night to find your computer covered with Kool-Aid your kindergarten-aged daughter spilled, you can rest assured that your handouts, lessons, quizzes, and retests are all safely stored online *and* on the other machines that you use regularly. Shared folders in Google Drive can be even more valuable, however, to members of learning teams. Content that individual team members create becomes instantly accessible to everyone when peers who work closely give each other access to the content stored in their Google Drive—a simple step that can be taken when setting up folders on each device. Here's why that matters: when the resources your peers use to teach common concepts become instantly available to you, the time, energy, and effort that it takes to work together are reduced.

Google Drive does more than simply provide users with the ability to maintain synced folders together. Users of Google Drive also have access to Google Docs, Sheets, Forms, and Slides—online applications that facilitate the creation of a wide range of common work products. Google Docs is a word processor used to generate text-based files that can be edited in the same ways that you would edit files in Microsoft Word. Google Sheets is a tool that allows users to collect and manipulate data sets, mirroring the functionality of Microsoft Excel. Google Forms makes it possible to create and deliver surveys to audiences, automatically dropping responses into new Google Sheets for review, and users of Google Slides can create the kinds of presentations Microsoft PowerPoint popularized. All of these applications allow users to export and save final products in more common file types—think DOC, XLSX, PPT, and PDF—ensuring that the work done in Google is easy to translate in settings that still rely on Microsoft Office for generating new content.

What makes Google Docs, Sheets, Forms, and Slides different is that users can collaborate with one another around common work products in *real time*. That means members of your learning team can revise and edit shared content simultaneously during your regularly scheduled meetings. To develop a common formative assessment, create a new file in Google Docs and start writing. One group of teachers can work on multiple-choice questions while another generates a few novel performance tasks for students to tackle. Planning to use a PowerPoint presentation to review key vocabulary at the end of an important lesson? Create a new file in Google Slides and start writing. One group of teachers can craft definitions for each word while another inserts images to use as examples of the new term in action. Interested in surveying your students about a recent instructional practice? Create a new file in Google Forms and start writing. One group of teachers can think through the kinds of demographic data that you will want to collect in order to make your data set useful while another can develop questions designed to elicit meaningful feedback from your students. *Every revision* to your shared file is instantly saved and instantly viewable by *every person* on your collaborative team.

No longer will members get lost in revised versions of common documents. Anyone can make changes to sets of essential outcomes, polish the language on common assessments, and add exemplars to shared rubrics because everyone has access to the most recent versions of team files in his or her Google Drive. When time that was once wasted in frustrating searches for the latest versions of shared content is recaptured, the collaborative production of content becomes an easy practice to embrace.

Google Drive isn't the only digital service that makes it possible for teams of teachers to maintain shared folders with one another. Another popular tool offering similar functionality is Dropbox (www .dropbox.com). Like Google Drive, Dropbox syncs content saved in a specific folder to both the web and to multiple devices. New files and revisions to existing files are uploaded to the web automatically and downloaded to other devices instantly. Dropbox folders can also be shared with other users, allowing collaborative teams to house ever-changing—and ever-updated—collections of content produced together. While Dropbox doesn't provide access to content creation tools like Google Drive or make it possible for multiple users to collaborate around the same document in real time, many teachers find the syncing features of Dropbox to be more sophisticated and seamless than those Google provides.

Regardless of the service that you choose to embrace, the following tips can help your learning team manage collaborative production efforts more effectively.

Create a Common Naming Structure for Files in Shared Folders

Shared folders for team-based content have been a common organizing practice in PLCs for years. However, shared folders are only useful when learning teams work together to define a common naming structure for the files that individual teachers are likely to add to shared collections. Start by thinking through the types of content that you typically create for one another—quizzes, tests, handouts, readings, presentations, labs, study guides, rubrics. Then commit to adding a short label that specifies the content type to the beginning of each file's name when creating new materials. Doing so will automatically sort files in shared folders by category, making it easier for other members of your team to spot useful content quickly. (See table 2.1, page 30, for an example.)

Table 2.1: Creating a Common Naming Structure for a Shared Folder

Shared Folder of a Learning Team *Without* a Common Naming Structure for Files	Shared Folder of a Learning Team *With* a Common Naming Structure for Files
Ancient Egypt Government Quiz Comparing the Greeks to the Egyptians Egyptian Mythology Project Farming in Ancient Egypt Hammurabi's Code Test Rubric for Mythology Project The Fertile Crescent Vocabulary for Ancient Egypt Who Was Ra?	Assessment_Ancient Egyptian Government Assessment_Hammurabi's Code Handout_Farming in Ancient Egypt PowerPoint_Ancient Egypt Vocabulary Project_Comparing the Greeks to the Egyptians Project_Egyptian Mythology Reading_The Fertile Crescent Reading_Who Was Ra? Rubric_Egyptian Mythology Project

Create Templates for Common Document Types

To make the collaborative production of shared content even more efficient and effective, successful learning teams also create templates for common document types. Deciding on a structure for content that teachers may develop on their own means that members will spend less time trying to figure out how to use materials their peers create. Templates for activities might include places for brief descriptions of the sequence of instruction, background knowledge students should understand before tackling the task, and extensions for students who need remediation, enrichment, or both. Templates for rubrics might include predetermined criteria and language that describe levels of student mastery. Templates for quick formative assessments may set aside space for student corrections, reflections, or both.

Set Aside Time to Clean Out Shared Folders

Just like the bookmark collections described in chapter 1, shared folders containing team resources need regular maintenance. Setting aside time each month to clean out shared folders—deleting files that are no longer relevant, revising files in need of polishing, adding files with potential that were created on the fly—can build momentum for the collaborative production of content simply because it increases the odds that teachers will find useful resources every time they turn to a team's shared folder.

Maintaining shared collections of resources is one of the most productive steps that learning teams can take with one another. Sharing content saves everyone time. More importantly, sharing content helps members of individual learning teams coordinate their work. Both practices are fundamentally important in professional learning communities. It is also essential, however, for teams to develop systems and structures that enable sharing *beyond* the learning team.

Sharing Beyond Your Learning Team

While tools like Google Drive, Google Docs, and Dropbox can make the collaborative production and sharing of content *within* your learning team easy, it is important to remember that there are people *beyond* your learning team who could benefit from having access to the materials that you are creating. Finding ways to make your content accessible to the special educators supporting your students during remediation and enrichment periods—the encore teachers willing to partner with you to create truly integrated learning experiences—and the peers working in the same content area at different grade levels helps coordinate the efforts of everyone in your PLC by building a shared awareness of the content covered in every classroom. In many ways, wikis are the best digital tool for facilitating this kind of school-level coordination.

Wikis—a term that comes from the Hawaiian word for *fast*— are easy-to-edit websites. While there is nothing flashy about wikis, they are the perfect digital tool for facilitating group collaboration because they are approachable to everyone—including teachers with little technical skill. Once users are given permission to work on a shared wiki, they can click an edit button found on every page to add and delete content. Users are then shown menus and toolbars similar to those found in common word-processing applications. Font styles and colors can be changed, bulleted and numbered lists can be created, links to external content can be inserted, video content can be embedded, important files can be uploaded, and additional pages can be added. Changes in most wiki services save automatically. In other services, users manually click a button when they finish to save any changes they make.

From an internal standpoint, what the sixth-grade science teachers at Salem Middle School in Apex, North Carolina, like about their wiki (http://6sci.pbworks.com) is the fact that their resources are accessible from any computer connected to the Internet, making it possible for teachers to add content and draw from the expertise of their colleagues whether they are working at school or at home. For a team used to posting content for one another in a shared folder on its school's server, this flexibility is a welcome change. No longer do teachers have to remember to move resources created after hours onto the school's server when returning to school. Instead, they can post content immediately, eliminating a barrier to efficient and effective sharing. Externally, though, their wiki has become a powerful communication tool. Because content is organized by unit and because the team has chosen to include written descriptions of the role that individual resources play in supporting instruction, anyone can scan the team's wiki to get a sense of the content covered in sixth-grade science. Gaining the collaborative support of practitioners working in other departments or grade levels now starts by simply pointing people to their wiki.

Two of the most popular wiki services are PBworks (www.pbworks .com) and Wikispaces (www.wikispaces.com). Both offer free, basic accounts to educators that are more than capable of housing all of the resources a learning team creates; both make editing content easy for anyone, regardless of technical skill; and both allow teachers to create free accounts for students—making it possible to integrate wiki work into classroom instruction. Choosing the right wiki tool for your learning team, then, becomes a matter of personal preference. Start by asking if any of your peers or professional contacts has embraced one service over the other. Tapping into connections with folks who have found a product that they love means you are more likely to get support whenever you are struggling to make a tool work. Also, touch base with members of your district's instructional technology team. They can help you determine whether the features and functionalities individual services offer align with district policies and protocols—an important consideration whenever you are working to integrate new tools into your work.

Regardless of which service you pick, the following tips can help you build a wiki that will be useful to everyone.

Remember Wikis Are Public Places to Store the Shared Content Your Team Is Creating Together

The best way to think about the role that wikis can play in supporting cooperation in PLCs is to imagine them as a replacement for the shared folder that learning teams have traditionally used to organize the content that they are creating together. Your learning team doesn't *create* content in a shared folder, and neither should it create content in a wiki. Instead, your learning team should *store* the content that you have created elsewhere in a wiki. Turn your wiki into a public warehouse—a place where anyone interested in supporting your students can find a collection of quality resources that can be used in his or her daily work.

Add Short Written Descriptions to Every Piece of Content Posted

Tapping into the full potential of the professionals working beyond your learning team starts by recognizing that those professionals—special educators, instructional support teachers, elective teachers, school administrators—won't always have a nuanced understanding of your curriculum or the instructional resources that you are creating together. Adding two- or three-sentence descriptions to every piece of content stored in your wiki—explanations of the essential outcomes for important units, details about how to use individual handouts, overviews of the role that external websites can play in teaching required objectives—can build both the background knowledge and expertise of practitioners who aren't full-time members of your learning team or full-time experts in your curriculum.

Adding short written descriptions to all of the content posted in your wiki also increases the efficiency of *everyone* using your shared resources. No longer do teachers—whether they are working on or off an individual learning team—have to guess at the purpose of materials shared by their peers. Instead, they can quickly determine whether or not an individual resource is worth exploring before ever opening the file. That saves time, and saving time is an essential first step toward ensuring the collaborative production of content becomes common practice in your learning community.

Add Links to Files Created in Services Like Google Drive or Dropbox to Your Wiki

Both Google Drive and Dropbox allow users instant access to the latest version of any shared file no matter how many times it is revised. Both services also allow users to create public web links that point directly to individual files. Consider adding these links to your wiki instead of uploading final copies of documents to resource pages in your learning team's wiki. Linking to files stored in shared folders instead of uploading static versions of the same files guarantees that anyone looking at resources in your wiki will have access to the latest revisions of everything that you are producing together. You can also eliminate one of the most time-consuming tasks involved in managing a team-based wiki: uploading new versions of existing documents your learning team creates.

Settle on a Predetermined Structure for Organizing Content

Making sure that your wiki remains useful starts by settling on a predetermined structure for how to organize the content you want to share. Will you create a separate page in your wiki for each of the units that you are responsible for teaching? What kinds of content do you generally create for each unit? Is some of that content more important than others? Does it make sense for that content to appear first on individual unit pages in your wiki so that it can be found easily? Making these decisions together and then creating blank templates for individual pages complete with subtitles in advance guarantees that your final wiki will be organized logically *and* consistently—a key to efficient navigation.

Assign Monitoring Responsibilities to Individual Teachers

Like every other tool referenced so far in this text, team wikis require regular monitoring and maintenance. New files, pages housing materials, and links to useful web-based sources need to be added, and old files, pages, and links need to be removed. Divide responsibility for this regular maintenance early in your wiki work. Maybe each member of your team can be responsible for updating one unit page or one content type on your wiki. Then, set time aside in regularly scheduled meetings for teachers to polish the content that they are responsible for monitoring. Investing time in managing your wiki will save everyone time later.

Leave Wikis Open for Viewing to Facilitate Cooperation Beyond Your Learning Team

Like most digital tools, wikis allow users to apply a broad range of access or edit permissions to any content that is created. Individual pages, files, and folders in a wiki can be completely open to viewing or accessible only to specific users who sign in with passwords. That means teams who are concerned about providing too much access to their shared materials can make careful choices about what they want to make public and what they want to keep private.

A word of warning, however: every time that you lock content behind a password, you create a new barrier to cooperation. If you decide that common assessments shouldn't be public because you are worried about the potential of students finding them on the web, you now need to create usernames and passwords for special programs teachers who want to help students to study for upcoming tests. If you lock your whole site behind a password because you are concerned about folks critiquing or criticizing your work, you may inadvertently lock out potential partners who can help you to improve your practice. While the privacy of a password can make us feel safe, leaving everything on your wiki open for viewing removes barriers to cooperation—and removing barriers to cooperation is a good thing in a learning community.

Conclusion

As collaborative groups spend more time together, they develop both the will and the skill to tackle increasingly complex tasks. This shift often begins when teams move from *sharing ideas* to *sharing intentions* with one another—and while sharing intentions with one another aligns nicely with the core motivations that drive human beings, it is no easy task. "Cooperating is harder than simply sharing," Shirky (2008) writes, "because it involves changing your behavior to synchronize with people who are changing their behaviors to synchronize with you" (Kindle location 684).

Synchronizing on learning teams depends on teachers who are willing to negotiate with one another. Choices about what students need to know and be able to do are no longer left to individuals. Similarly, synchronization in professional learning communities depends on teachers who are willing to collaboratively produce content together. Common assessments become a tangible expression of what the individual members of learning teams believe in, and core lessons are a reflection of the expertise of the group.

Previously, the transaction costs associated with this kind of professional synchronization have limited the effectiveness of learning communities. Successfully negotiating with one another and producing, organizing, and sharing content together may sound great in theory, but the benefits of negotiations and the collaborative production of content have always been outweighed by the time, energy, and effort necessary to translate these cooperative behaviors into action. For learning teams open to integrating digital tools into their practice, however, cooperation—both within and beyond the learning team—becomes possible.

Chapter 3
Taking Collective Action

Belarusian leader Alexander Lukashenko is often described as Europe's last dictator. He has relied on heavy-handed practices to silence political opposition since rising to the presidency of the Eastern European nation after the fall of the Soviet Union in 1994. Free speech is almost nonexistent in Belarus, and presidential elections are a sham. Opposing candidates are regularly arrested and jailed alongside their supporters multiple times each campaign season. Not surprisingly, Lukashenko wins reelection every four years, earning such a high percentage of the popular vote that outside observers—and Belarusian dissenters—are convinced that the ballot totals are rigged (BelarusDigest, 2014; Fletcher, 2014).

If ever there was a place where collective action—identifying a shared desire and then tackling a challenging task together—is needed, it's Belarus. However, standing up to Lukashenko has proven to be nearly impossible. Opposing political parties are allowed to exist, but they are not allowed to play any role in the Belarusian parliament. Prior governmental approval is required for all public assemblies, and participation in unlawful assemblies results in fines and short prison terms. Military police stand ready to break up any protest, often using unnecessarily harsh levels of force in an attempt to discourage future action. The most influential opponents to Lukashenko's power can be imprisoned for years for simply questioning the legitimacy of election results or drawing attention to injustice (BelarusDigest, 2014).

Previously, crushing dissent has been easy for Lukashenko. Creating public broadcast messages that criticize the actions of the government is impossible in a nation where the state controls all of the radio stations, newspapers, and television channels. Citizens savvy enough to throw up websites in an effort to bypass state-run media sources are subject to relentless attacks from state-sponsored hackers. Advertising a public protest puts you on the radar of the police, who are more than willing to show up and take everyone to jail (BelarusDigest, 2014).

However, a clever series of demonstrations in the wake of the contested 2006 presidential election started to change the way that people organize in Belarus. In May 2006, an anonymous blogger created a short post encouraging dissenters to meet in the capital city's largest public square to do nothing other than eat ice cream. Predictably, the government saw these plans as a form of unlawful assembly and turned out the police to put an end to the "protest." The result: dozens of Belarusians enjoying ice cream together on a beautiful spring day were arrested by cops in riot gear. Things were different this time, however. The protesters—armed with cell phones and Internet connections—began uploading pictures and video of the police actions that spread quickly across the web, grabbing the attention of the world community (Carvin, 2006; Shirky, 2008).

Because of the success of the so-called Ice Cream Revolution, dissenters organized additional impromptu protests. Text messages and blog posts drawing attention to the demonstrations were forwarded from one cell phone to the next, rapidly spreading word across the country. All of these events resulted in similar crackdowns.

Additionally, these events resulted in similar public embarrassment for Belarus as protesters used digital devices to quickly share evidence of the government's absurd reaction to seemingly innocuous gatherings—including a day where dissenters spent the afternoon walking around a public square *smiling* at one another, only to be arrested by police (Shirky, 2008). For Lukashenko, the game had changed. Digital tools made it possible for protesters to organize without formal organization. Lukashenko quickly learned that he couldn't stop events planned without significant prior planning or avoid public ridicule and condemnation for coercive attempts to silence citizens when video of riot police arresting smiling Belarusians could be uploaded to the web instantly.

You see the lesson in the Belarusian story, don't you? We are *all* tuned into collective action—but only when that collective action seems feasible. Standing up to Lukashenko in 1994 required too much effort and carried too many consequences to capture the attention of a significant proportion of the Belarusian population. Add digital tools to the mix, however—something that didn't happen until cell phones with cheap text messaging plans, built-in cameras, and wireless Internet connections saturated the Belarusian telecommunications marketplace—and seizing the hearts and minds of a nation becomes possible. "Whenever you improve a group's ability to communicate internally," Shirky (2008) writes, "you change the things it is capable of" (Kindle location 2132).

However, digital tools aren't just changing what political activists are capable of. Digital tools can also change the things that your professional learning community is capable of. Building a genuinely shared sense of mission and vision and tracking progress by student and standard—core behaviors that were once too difficult to truly take hold in our schools and systems—can become the norm rather than the exception to the rule if you are willing to examine the role that technology plays in facilitating collective action.

Collective Action Depends on Cohesion

Unlike sharing or cooperating, taking collective action is only possible when members of a group are genuinely committed to achieving a better future together. Collective action begins when the will of the group becomes more important than the individual wills of its members. That makes it the most complicated collaborative behavior to master: "All group structures create dilemmas, but these dilemmas are hardest when it comes to collective action, because the cohesion of the group becomes critical to its success" (Shirky, 2008, Kindle location 702).

Cohesion in any group depends on developing a shared mission and vision that taps into a greater moral purpose. The answers to questions like "What do we believe in?," "Why does our work matter?," and "What do we hope the results of our shared efforts will be?" become the centering point for collective action, convincing individual members to set aside personal goals in favor of moving forward together. Why are Belarusian citizens willing to risk arrest by joining protests that they know police will monitor? Because standing up to injustice is more important than their safety. Why do thousands of individual writers make contributions to Wikipedia every year without getting anything in return? Because they know that together, they are creating an incredible resource that is available to everyone for free.

Richard DuFour and Robert Eaker (1998) write about the role that a shared mission and vision play in building cohesion and coordinating collective action in professional learning communities:

> When educators have a clear sense of purpose, direction, and the ideal future state of their school, they are better able to understand their ongoing roles within the school. This clarity simplifies the decision-making process and empowers all members of the staff to act with greater confidence. Rather than constantly checking with their bosses for approval, employees

> can simply ask, "Is this decision or action in line with the vision?" and then act on their own. (p. 84)

Yet building a shared mission and vision in PLCs has never been easy simply because building a shared mission and vision depends on giving *everyone* the chance to wrestle with powerful questions about teaching and learning *together*—and wrestling with powerful questions about teaching and learning takes time that schools don't always have. Instead of spending faculty meetings and staff-development days defining an ideal future for our schools, we struggle instead to respond to outside pressures that take priority, such as testing results the local paper publishes, district initiatives the new superintendent introduces, and state-level policy requirements with set deadlines.

That's where digital tools for facilitating asynchronous conversations can help. Are you struggling to bring everyone together for a discussion about the specific skills that today's students need to master in order to succeed in tomorrow's world? Trying to build a more responsible grading and homework policy but convinced that setting aside thirty minutes at an upcoming early release day will get you nowhere? Getting the sense that important voices are choosing to remain silent on critical issues simply because your faculty's main priority after a long day's work is seeing after-school meetings end early? Consider using a service like VoiceThread (http://voicethread .com) to start the conversations online and encourage teachers to make contributions whenever—and from wherever—they can.

In a practical sense, VoiceThread conversations are built like PowerPoint presentations. Users upload slides filled with provocative quotes, images, and video clips that can serve as starting points for dialogue. Once a collection of slides has been assembled into a single set and published to the web, text, voice, or video comments can be added to the developing thread. Conversations can be kept private—available for viewing and commenting by invitation only— or can be made public. Icons indicating that new comments have been added to conversations appear in the sidebar of every slide and are outlined in yellow, making it possible for participants to easily discover new content on return visits.

Visit http://bit.ly/gradingdebate to access an example of a Voice-Thread conversation about effective grading practices in professional learning communities. Notice that seven different quotes have been uploaded to spark initial thinking. Some of those quotes clearly resonated, eliciting more comments and conversation from participants. Also notice that participants have chosen to share their thinking in different ways. Some added text comments anonymously to the conversation while others added audio comments using their own names. Throughout, commenters responded and reacted to one another and to the initial prompt. This kind of public reflection is essential to articulating a shared vision that can be used to build the cohesion necessary for collective action.

What makes asynchronous conversations held in digital spaces powerful is that everyone has equal opportunities to get involved. New teachers—or teachers new to a school—aren't afraid of isolating themselves by sharing controversial ideas or challenging the notions of influential colleagues in front of everyone at traditional faculty meetings; staff members who are introverted or who need time to process can comfortably participate in conversations held online; and administrators who are struggling to ensure that their core beliefs haven't been inadvertently misinterpreted can carefully articulate their thinking in a public space.

Unlike staff meetings and professional development sessions, asynchronous conversations are not time dependent. That is important simply because conversations designed to build cohesion around core beliefs won't always fit into neat segments on your next meeting agenda—and whether they will admit it or not, every member of your staff is constantly making calculations about whether adding new contributions to faculty conversations is going to cause meetings to run longer than scheduled. That reticence to participate in the development of a shared vision can be crippling to professional learning communities. Time becomes the variable, however, in schools that embrace asynchronous conversations. People are more likely to participate when they know that they can participate before school, during planning periods, or after putting their kids to bed at night.

Finally, asynchronous conversations provide a tangible record of the will of the group. Principals no longer have to guess at how their faculties feel about important issues; teachers no longer have to wonder about whether their core beliefs mirror those of peers in other grade levels; and skeptics, critics, and curmudgeons can no longer undermine the forward progress of a school by arguing that shared decisions really aren't shared. Transparency is essential in groups determined to act together, and asynchronous conversations bring a measure of permanent transparency to conversations that traditional faculty meetings simply can't provide.

The following tips can help you successfully integrate asynchronous conversations into the collaborative practices of your learning community.

Use Asynchronous Conversations as Starting Points for Face-to-Face Faculty Discussions

Remember that asynchronous conversations are intended to supplement—not replace—face-to-face dialogue in your professional learning community. If there is an important issue that you need your teachers to come to consensus around, consider encouraging your teachers to share their thinking with one another in a VoiceThread conversation for a short period of time *before* your next faculty meeting. Then, start your meeting with reflections around the ideas posted in the online conversation. Ask your teachers to identify comments that they agree with, that challenge their thinking, and that they want to know more about. Doing so can move your conversation forward faster simply because staff members have the opportunity to interact with ideas and wrestle with their own opinions before your meeting even begins.

Make it Possible to Participate in Asynchronous Conversations Anonymously

For many school leaders, allowing staff members to add anonymous comments to asynchronous conversations in public spaces like VoiceThread can seem unreasonably risky. After all, it is entirely possible for unhappy staff members to post negative comments attacking initiatives or expressing opposition to core beliefs that the majority shares. The greater risk, however, is that reasonable members of your faculty will shy away from raising potentially controversial ideas in spaces where they are required to use their names while posting. Remember that consensus can't be reached if you aren't hearing from everyone—and hearing from everyone means doing everything that you can to encourage participation, including giving people the choice to tie their names to their thoughts or to remain anonymous.

Invite Other Important Stakeholders to Be a Part of Asynchronous Conversations

The chances are good that despite your best efforts, you have struggled to get people like parents, business owners, and religious and community-organization leaders involved in the development of your school's mission and vision. The simple truth is that it is just as difficult for important stakeholders working beyond your building to find the time to join your conversations as it is for you to find the time to invite them to the table. So make your asynchronous discussions public and invite everyone to join your staff while you work to develop a shared sense for what really matters to the people in your community. Even if only a small handful of folks contribute to the discussion, those contributions can help ensure that your vision is an accurate reflection of the expectations that your community has for your school.

Building a shared mission and vision provides an essential foundation for groups of individuals who are ready to work together. By serving as a de facto filter for decision making, a shared mission and vision can provide direction for everyone. Once collaborative groups have a sense of where they want to go together, it is time to take collective action.

Use of Digital Tools to Facilitate Collective Action Around Student Learning

Members of professional learning communities understand that collective strength is more important than individual talent when it comes to meeting the needs of every student. Richard DuFour, Rebecca DuFour, Robert Eaker, and Thomas Many (2010) write,

> The idea so frequently heard in schools—"These are *my* kids, *my* room, and *my* materials"—must give way to a new paradigm of "These are *our* kids and we cannot help all of them learn without a collective effort." (pp. 104–105)

As learning teams mature, then, they center their collaborative efforts on taking collective action to ensure that *every* student masters essential outcomes, no matter what.

Taking collective action to ensure that every student masters essential outcomes is no easy task. It depends on a learning team's ability to collect concrete evidence of student learning. As response to intervention experts Austin Buffum, Mike Mattos, and Chris Weber (2012) explain,

> The solution to helping all students achieve success doesn't come in a box. It comes when collaborative teams gather ongoing, detailed information, as a part of instruction, to effectively identify students who need additional time and support in their current grade-level curriculum. Through the use of these data, teachers can identify exactly which students have not mastered

> specific essential standards; determine the specific
> needs of each child, subsequently matching each
> student's need to the appropriate instruction and inter-
> vention; and monitor the student's response. In other
> words, assessment data must describe student prog-
> ress *by the student, by the standard, by the learning
> target.* (p. 109, italics in original)

The challenge in collecting assessment data that describe progress by student, by standard, and by learning target lies in the
fact that too many of today's teachers are still doing this complex
work manually. Imagine the complexity of learning from data sets
detailing the mastery levels of large groups of students using nothing more than data notebooks or exit slips collected at the end
of every class period. Try disaggregating the results of common
assessments when "disaggregating" means looking for patterns in
lists of student scores maintained on clipboards or in stacks of
papers sorted by class period. *Collective action* is impossible when
simply *collecting data* becomes an overwhelming task. That's where
digital tools like MasteryConnect (www.masteryconnect.com) and
Global PD (www.globalpd.com) can help. Designed to automate
the collecting, recording, and reporting of data in PLCs, both tools
make it possible for teachers to spend more time on the kinds of
high-leverage practices—identifying students in need of intensive
interventions, spotting effective instructional practices, regrouping
students for remediation and enrichment—that really *can* ensure
that every student succeeds.

After creating a free basic account, MasteryConnect users can
import student rosters and create gradebooks called Trackers for
individual class periods. Then, users can upload and deliver their
own common assessments or look for new assessments worth
delivering in MasteryConnect's Assessment Library. What makes
MasteryConnect uniquely valuable to learning teams is that while
preparing an assessment for delivery, users are required to identify the standard *every* question assesses. This encourages responsible practice, allowing teams to identify standards that they are

emphasizing or inadvertently ignoring on common assessments. More importantly, spotting patterns in data sets becomes possible when every question on every assessment is tied directly to an individual standard. As assessments are delivered and student responses are recorded—a process that can be conducted by holding paper bubble sheets in front of webcams for instant scoring in classrooms with limited technology *or* by asking students to take tests online in classrooms with lots of technology—color-coded spreadsheets organized by both student and standard are automatically updated. Trying to find specific standards that students are struggling to master? Look for columns shaded red in your Tracker. Want to know which students are ready for enrichment? Their results will be shaded green in your Tracker.

For users with basic accounts, sharing results with colleagues, parents, and practitioners working beyond the classroom is a matter of printing out individual assessment reports and bringing them to meetings. Pay for MasteryConnect's premium features, however, and results can be automatically shared with anyone who is interested. Parents can access reports detailing the standards that their students are struggling to master as well as quick instructional tutorials pulled from online libraries like Khan Academy (www.khanacademy.org) that can be used for review; learning teams can sort through results that are disaggregated by teacher, making it possible to identify practitioners who have discovered instructional practices with potential; and district-level leaders can pinpoint pockets of exceptional practice within their systems that are worth exploring and amplifying.

Global PD—a subscription product developed by Solution Tree—provides users with similar functionality. Common assessments can be created, delivered, and scored instantly in Global PD; results can be sorted by both student and standard; and reports indicating teachers who have identified instructional practices worth pursuing can be generated automatically. Global PD is different from MasteryConnect, however, in that it provides extensive supports to teams that are still learning to use assessments as tools for driving collective action. Global PD pulls in Solution Tree resources—videos from experts, handouts from books, and protocols from professional learning community collections—that you can use immediately.

Nothing about the notion of working together to provide remediation and enrichment to students is hard to understand. However, there is a difference between *understanding* the importance of working together to meet the unique needs of every student and *believing* that working together to meet the unique needs of every student is actually possible. Using digital tools like MasteryConnect and Global PD to automate the most time-consuming data collection and management practices can certainly increase the likelihood that the teachers in your professional learning community take collective action around student learning data. Taking collective action around student learning data, however, depends on more than digital tools that automatically disaggregate assessment results. Taking collective action also depends on:

- **Clear protocols for making data conversations safe**—While digital tools can make it possible to spot trends and patterns in student learning data without difficulty, conversations between peers around just what those trends and patterns mean are never easy. Teachers confronted with evidence of the impact that their practices are having on students can feel uneasy about—even intimidated by—standing transparently in front of their peers. Successfully moving beyond this professional tension depends on your willingness to introduce clear protocols and processes for structuring data conversations alongside any new digital tools designed to make it easier for learning teams to collect and manipulate data. Teachers are far more likely to use student learning data to take action together once they are convinced that data conversations can be easy *and* safe.

- **A firm understanding of what meaningful assessment looks like in action**—Determined to save time, energy, and effort, learning teams that embrace digital tools for data collection can inadvertently slip into the habit of using multiple-choice questions—the type of questions that services like MasteryConnect and Global PD can score easily—to assess everything. Integrating essays and performance tasks into common assessments can seem like a chore to teams that have been spoiled by the simplicity of services that automatically build data sets from multiple-choice questions. Avoiding these uncomfortable patterns depends on your ability to think beyond the bubble. What kinds of questions will you have to cut from your current assessments if you rely on digital tools to grade everything for you? Would cutting those questions mean that you are failing to assess more complex bits of knowledge and skills? Are there ways that digital tools could help you record progress toward mastering higher-order skills? Could you use digital tools to collect self-assessment data from students or to organize the results of work scored against rubrics? However you answer these questions, make sure that your team isn't settling for assessing just the things that are easy to assess.

- **The professional flexibility to experiment with intervening across a hallway**—Having digital tools for organizing and manipulating data is only the first step toward facilitating collective action around student learning in a PLC. Working together to intervene on behalf of students in need of remediation or enrichment also depends on having the professional flexibility to experiment with new instructional structures. Do your teachers have permission to adjust their class schedules to regroup students across an entire hallway? Are there plans in your building to create a schoolwide intervention period yet? Until the time and flexibility exist within the regular school day for teams and teachers to work together to address identified student learning needs, data will remain useless as a tool for organizing collective action.

Conclusion

Like the work of all collaborative groups, teacher learning teams can't reach their full potential until they begin to take action together. As school change expert Cassandra Erkens (2008) argues,

> Professional learning communities engage in inquiry regarding their own effectiveness; they challenge the status quo; they generate collective responses to students who aren't learning; and ultimately, they transform their understanding of education and their capacity as teachers who impact learning. All of that work involves risk taking on behalf of the community and encouragement on behalf of administrators. (p. 49)

That work depends on more than just risk taking, though. That work depends on building intellectual cohesion across your faculty. Using digital tools to facilitate asynchronous conversations can help embed core beliefs in the hearts and minds of people throughout your school community by creating a concrete reminder of everything that you believe in together.

That work also depends on reducing the transaction costs tied to taking collective action. Engaging in inquiry regarding individual effectiveness, challenging the status quo, generating collective responses to students who aren't learning, and transforming our capacity as teachers who impact learning are all core behaviors that digital tools can support.

Epilogue:
Change Starts With
Unlearning the Obvious

When Johannes Gutenberg developed his movable type printing press in 1439, he was challenging traditional publishing and communication patterns. Instead of operating under the assumption that books had to be painstakingly produced by hand and available only to the elite—the norm in Western Europe at the time—Gutenberg believed that printing could be automated, books could be affordable, and everyone could be literate. So he borrowed from two existing ideas—wood-block printing first developed in China and Korea and screw-type wine presses common in the Rhine Valley—to design a tool that reduced the time, energy, and effort attached to publishing (Newitz, 2012). Gutenberg's press meant that for the first time, ideas could be copied and shared quickly, and as ordinary people found themselves increasingly surrounded by text, they learned to read. This newfound access to information changed the world by making it possible for large numbers of people to tap into the basic human need to share, cooperate, and take action together.

Gutenberg's press was only the first of many changes to the ways we communicate. Soon after printed text became common, Venetian printer Aldus Manutius began to publish works that resembled today's paperback books in an attempt to make personal libraries—and by default, the ideas they contained—portable (Shirky, 2008). In the early 1800s, the printing process was mechanized, eliminating the need for workers to press individual pages by hand; by the mid-1800s, self-feeding presses were developed, eliminating the need to hand-feed paper while printing; and by the late 1800s, the linotype machine—a typewriter that sent lines of text to be immediately cast in hot metal—was invented, eliminating the need to set casts for pages by hand (Harry Ransom Center, n.d.). The very notion of publishing itself has been redefined in the last hundred years, moving from a task corporate giants exclusively tackled to a task that anyone with access to the Internet can tackle. Whether we were using typewriters, home computers, laser printers, or personal websites or blogs, new tools and technologies have made it possible for *everyone* to share ideas and build audiences (Godin, 2010).

Taken as a whole, the changes in the way that content is produced and consumed have been nothing short of revolutionary. The monks working to copy manuscripts in the scriptoriums of the Middle Ages could never have imagined a world where the ability to read—let alone publish—was nearly universal. Yet looking back, each change in the way that content is produced and consumed—making smaller versions of larger texts, using machines instead of humans to press pages, developing printers that can feed their own paper, creating personal devices for publishing—was the logical next step. Acting on those logical next steps, however, depended on people willing to *unlearn the obvious*, the key trait that defines innovators who drive meaningful change (Shirky, 2008). Gutenberg had to believe that everyone wanted to read before he could move forward with his plans for a printing press; Manutius had to believe that people wanted to carry their libraries with them before he could move forward with his plans to produce smaller books; and Tim Berners-Lee had to believe that there were real reasons that people would want to communicate across borders before he could move forward with his plans to develop the World Wide Web.

Look carefully at the stories that start each chapter in *How to Use Digital Tools to Support Teachers in a PLC*, and you will see additional examples of unlearning the obvious in action. The founders of Flickr had to believe that people actually wanted to share their personal photographs openly before they could design a service that has fundamentally changed how images are used; Jimmy Wales and Larry Sanger had to believe that complete strangers would be willing to cooperate to create a reliable, open-source encyclopedia before they could develop Wikipedia; and Belarusian protesters had to believe that enough people in the world would care about the conditions in their country before they could take collective action to document the heavy-handed tactics of their government.

Unless you were just born, your personal life is full of examples of unlearning the obvious. As Shirky (2008) explains,

> I know that newspapers are where you get your political news and how you look for a job. I know that music comes from stores. I know that if you want to have a conversation with someone, you call them on the phone. I know that complicated things like software or encyclopedias have to be created by professionals. In the last fifteen years, I've had to unlearn every one of those things and a million others because those things stopped being true. (Kindle location 3910)

The members of your school community are also going to have to unlearn the obvious if you are going to become a PLC. Teachers are going to have to believe that collaboration is worthwhile before they ever begin sharing resources; team members are going to have to believe that their peers have professional expertise worth learning from before they ever begin to produce shared lessons and common assessments; and your entire faculty is going to have to believe that every student is capable of mastering the knowledge and skills necessary to succeed in tomorrow's world before you can ever hope to take action together. Healthy PLCs depend on practitioners who are willing to push against the inertia of experience and challenge the notion that teaching is a solitary act.

Challenging these notions will be no easy task simply because the culture of isolation in education is so strong. The unfortunate truth is that the vast majority of teachers still work in schools like the one that Richard DuFour (2008) spent his early career working in.

> Our sharing stopped . . . at our respective classroom doors, because within our classrooms, each of us reigned supreme. I never had to concern myself with what content others were teaching, because each of us was free to determine his or her own curriculum. There was no process, expectation, or even encouragement for me to discuss with colleagues my curriculum pacing, my instructional strategies, the methods and rigor of my assessments, my homework policy, my grading practices, my response to students who struggled, or any other vital issues essential to effective teaching. The only thing my sections of our US History course had in common with the sections taught by others in my department was the title. (p. 1)

The good news is that—just like the evolutionary development of publishing and printing practices—the strategies and suggestions recommended in *How to Use Digital Tools to Support Teachers in a PLC* are likely to be logical next steps for teams who *are* willing to unlearn the obvious and embrace sharing, cooperating, and taking collective action. Why struggle alone to find valuable web-based content when you can use Diigo to work together to build a collection of resources that you know are worthwhile? Why struggle to figure out where revised versions of team files are saved on your personal computer when shared folders in Google Drive and Dropbox can give you instant access to the latest changes the moment they are made? Why struggle to track progress toward mastery of essential skills by student and by standard when MasteryConnect and Global PD can automate the entire process for you?

Better yet, encouraging teams to experiment with digital tools for sharing, cooperating, and taking collective action will leave them better prepared to integrate those same tools into their instruction. Are you convinced that it is essential for *students* to learn to filter and sort online information? If so, start by showing your *teachers* how digital tools for filtering and sorting information can make their lives easier. Are you ready to see *student groups* using digital tools to create shared reports and presentations? Then ask *teacher teams* to use digital tools to create content with each other. Are you certain that opportunities to build knowledge through collaborative dialogue in asynchronous conversations would benefit the *students* in your school? Then give your *teachers* the same opportunities as you work to articulate your school's mission and vision. Teachers who have firsthand experience with the role that digital tools can play in making learners more efficient and effective are far more likely to change their classroom practices than teachers who see technology integration as something that matters to students and students alone.

So where should your efforts to use digital tools to support sharing, cooperating, and taking collective action in a professional learning community begin? The answer is with the practices that will increase the efficiency and effectiveness of your learning team *right now.* Are you spending entire planning periods working through emails from peers sharing links to great websites? Social bookmarking is the right starting point. Has your principal required every team in your building to develop a common assessment for an upcoming unit? Then give the collaborative production of content a try. Do you think that your staff are struggling to work together because you lack cohesion? It might be time to embrace asynchronous conversations. Know that whatever starting point you choose, you will be strengthening the collaborative power of your professional learning community—and strengthening the collaborative power of professional learning communities is an outcome that we can *all* embrace.

References

Alexa. (2014, November 16). *The top 500 sites on the web.* Accessed at www.alexa.com/topsites on November 16, 2014.

BelarusDigest. (2014, July 3). Belarus mythbuster: What is it like to live in 'Europe's last dictatorship'? *The Guardian.* Accessed at www.theguardian.com/world/2014/jul/03/belarus-mythbuster -what-like-live-europe-last-dictatorship on November 16, 2014.

Buffum, A., Mattos, M., & Weber, C. (2012). *Simplifying response to intervention: Four essential guiding principles.* Bloomington, IN: Solution Tree Press.

Busteed, B. (2013, January 7). *The school cliff: Student engagement drops with each school year.* Accessed at www.gallup.com/opinion /gallup/170525/school-cliff-student-engagement-drops-school -year.aspx on October 10, 2014.

Carvin, A. (2006, May 15). Belarus, flash mobs and the ice cream revolution [Web log post]. Accessed at www.andycarvin.com /?p=1181 on November 16, 2014.

Coney Island USA. (n.d.). *The mermaid parade.* Accessed at www .coneyisland.com/programs/mermaid-parade on January 17, 2015.

DuFour, R. (2008). Introduction. In C. Erkens, C. Jakicic, L. G. Jessie, D. King, S. V. Kramer, T. W. Many, et al., *The collaborative teacher: Working together as a professional learning community* (pp. 1–8). Bloomington, IN: Solution Tree Press.

DuFour, R., DuFour, R., & Eaker, R. (n.d.). *A big picture look at professional learning communities* [Brochure]. Accessed at www .allthingsplc.info/files/uploads/brochure.pdf on November 16, 2014.

DuFour, R., DuFour, R., Eaker, R., & Many, T. (2010). *Learning by doing: A handbook for professional learning communities at work* (2nd ed.). Bloomington, IN: Solution Tree Press.

DuFour, R., & Eaker, R. (1998). *Professional learning communities at work: Best practices for enhancing student achievement.* Bloomington, IN: Solution Tree Press.

Erkens, C. (2008). Growing teacher leadership. In A. Buffum, C. Erkens, C. Hinman, S. B. Huff, L. G. Jessie, T. L. Martin, et al., *The collaborative administrator: Working together as a professional learning community* (pp. 39–53). Bloomington, IN: Solution Tree Press.

Fletcher, M. (2014, March 6). Belarus: Europe's secret state. *British GQ.* Accessed at www.gq-magazine.co.uk/comment/articles /2014–03/06/belarus-dictatorship-alexander-lukashenko on November 16, 2014.

Fullan, M. (2013). *Stratosphere: Integrating technology, pedagogy, and change knowledge.* Dons Mills, Ontario, Canada: Pearson.

Godin, S. (2010, August 23). Moving on [Web log post]. Accessed at http://sethgodin.typepad.com/seths_blog/2010/08/moving-on .html on November 22, 2014.

Graham, P., & Ferriter, B. (2008). One step at a time. *Journal for Staff Development, 29*(3), 38–42.

Harry Ransom Center. (n.d.). *Printing yesterday and today: Primary source education modules—The Gutenberg Bible.* Austin: The University of Texas at Austin.

Internet Live Stats. (2014, November 16). *Twitter usage statistics.* Accessed at www.internetlivestats.com/twitter-statistics on November 16, 2014.

National Governors Association Center for Best Practices & Council of Chief State School Officers. (2010). *Common Core State Standards.* Washington, DC: Authors.

Newitz, A. (2012, May 14). *Printed books existed nearly 600 years before Gutenberg's Bible.* Accessed at http://io9.com/5910249 /printed-books-existed-nearly-600-years-before-gutenbergs-bible on November 22, 2014.

NGSS Lead States. (2013). *Next Generation Science Standards: For states, by states.* Washington, DC: National Academies Press.

Partnership for 21st Century Skills. (2009, April 22). *Framework for 21st century learning.* Washington, DC: Author. Accessed at www .p21.org/our-work/p21-framework on July 20, 2009.

Schmoker, M. (2004, November 1). Start here for improving teaching. *The School Administrator.* Accessed at www.aasa.org /SchoolAdministratorArticle.aspx?id=10218 on November 16, 2014.

Shirky, C. (2008). *Here comes everybody: The power of organizing without organizations* [Kindle version]. New York: Penguin. Accessed at www.amazon.com.

Wikimedia Foundation. (2014, September 11). *English Wikipedia at a glance.* Accessed at http://stats.wikimedia.org/EN/SummaryEN .htm on November 16, 2014.

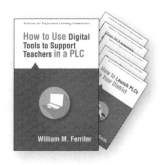

Solutions for Professional Learning Communities

The *Solutions Series* offers practitioners easy-to-implement recommendations on each book's topic—professional learning communities, digital classrooms, or modern learning. In a short, reader-friendly format, these how-to guides equip K–12 educators with the tools they need to take their school or district to the next level.

How to Use Digital Tools to Support Teachers in a PLC
William M. Ferriter
BKF675

How to Leverage PLCs for School Improvement
Sharon V. Kramer
BKF668

How to Coach Leadership in a PLC
Marc Johnson
BKF667

How to Develop PLCs for Singletons and Small Schools
Aaron Hansen
BKF676

How to Cultivate Collaboration in a PLC
Susan K. Sparks and Thomas W. Many
BKF678

How to Launch PLCs in Your District
W. Richard Smith
BKF665

"Tremendous, tremendous, tremendous!

The speaker made me do some very deep internal reflection about the **PLC process** and the personal responsibility I have in making the school improvement process work **for ALL kids.**"

—Marc Rodriguez, teacher effectiveness coach,
Denver Public Schools, Colorado

 PD Services

Our experts draw from decades of research and their own experiences to bring you practical strategies for building and sustaining a high-performing PLC. You can choose from a range of customizable services, from a one-day overview to a multiyear process.

Book your PLC PD today!
888.763.9045

Solution Tree